Fireflies

Poems of Love and Family

Keith Tornheim

Fireflies © 2016 Keith Tornheim. All rights reserved. Big Table Publishing Company retains the right to reprint. Permission to reprint must be obtained from the author, who owns the copyright.

ISBN: 978-0-9908413-8-8
Printed in the United States of America

Cover Design: CSRS

Some of these poems have previously appeared in the following:
Ibbetson Street: "A Good Walk" & "For Your Wedding"
The Somerville Times: "Fireflies" & "I Would Give You My Heart, But"

Also by Keith Tornheim:
Spoiled Fruit: Adam and Eve in Eden and Beyond

Big Table Publishing Company
Boston, MA
www.bigtablepublishing.com

Table of Contents

Fireflies	7
Apart	8
Attraction	9
One Year	10
Stockholm in September	11
Longing	12
Kiss Kiss	13
I Would Give You My Heart, But	14
On October 4, 2001	15
The Lump	16
After Thirty-Seven Years	17
Snore	18
Middle Ground	20
Closet Kiss	21
Pajama Pocket	22
Joint Account	23
Low-Lying Blankets	24
Just the Outside	25
Entwined from May to May	26
Island	27
The Bedouin Dress	28
A Good Walk	29
Why Flesh and Blood?	30
Daughters	32
KENDRA	34
Graduation Day 1997	35
Thirty-Three	36
To Kendra at Thirty-Seven	37
6-12	38
For Your Wedding	39

Wedding Day	40
KYLA	41
Blue-Eyed Bundle	42
May You Grow Old in Love	44
Baby Bellies	45
On First Holding My Grandson	46
Zichri Berel	47
Motherhood Suits You	48
Thunder Stick	49
Bequests to My Children	50

Dedicated to my wife Susan and our daughters Kendra and Kyla. They have provided me with so much more than poetic inspiration and an enthusiastic audience. I am eternally grateful for their love and support and our lives together, more than I can say, even with poetry.

Fireflies

Do you remember when
the summer skies were full of stars
and competing clouds of fireflies,
and we walked and talked
of everything
till kisses interrupted words?
In honor of that time,
now nearly fifty years ago,
each night before we go to sleep,
I reach an arm across the bed
to hold you close for just a moment;
then you present your lips
for that short kiss
that echoes years of longer ones.
Now we hope to sleep till dawn,
but we remember once
we walked all night through fireflies
to greet the next day's sun.

2012

Apart

We are together, though apart,
a thousand miles bridged by quiet thought,
each in our separate rooms, our separate selves,
remembering cities held in common:
The first glance of choice, concealed in a crowd;
a folk dance—the first walk toward dawn;
the first kiss—on the old stone steps;
the first tears of parting, and the next;
and after each long absence, a return
in the joy of refinding and being found.

1967

Attraction

Like a leaf to the light
I turned my face toward you,
reflecting smiles across a noise-filled room;
and again in quiet solemnity
when I gave you my ring and my promise;
when I held our firstborn in joy
and our second in wonder and pride;
in ten thousand nights and in the mornings
and at the mundane table;
in hugs of celebrations
and sometimes of grief.

You are my North Star.
You magnetized my heart,
and I come to unwavering rest
only after facing you.

2002

One Year

A year of being
more fully
together,
in postal address and social legality—
and above all, daily time—
has brought us a quietness.

The frantic rush of the river
when the dam is shattered
gives way to the slow, steady,
natural flow,
when the barriers have been down long
and forgotten.

Beneath the occasional ripples
of short words and hasty thoughts
moves the quiet power of walking
hand in hand.

1972

Stockholm in September

With the morning,
I stride briskly
(or is it flight?)
toward the urban kaleidoscope,
spun quickly to bedazzle
and distract.
See the glorious rooftops, turrets and spires,
      portholes eighty feet up!
See the carvings—caryatids and garlands!
See the water and the bridges and the boats,
urgent buses and taxis and trains!
(But don't hesitate too long in a quiet park.)

When I have walked hours of streets and shops,
a museum or two,
and at last the feet and back, dulled eye and head
say emphatically, "Enough!"
then I must return to the pleasant flat,
where every room is filled with your absence,
and none gives me sanctuary.

1996

Longing

In your shadowed absence, I am brittle.
I walk through molasses.
My breath is too much or too little.
There is no balance without your hand
to steady my pendulum,
to add counterpoint or harmonies.
The beat numbs; purpose is scattered.
The mouth of the cave beckons.
Sunlight is bleak, not warming,
the colors too jarring, or washed out.
My joys are shallow unshared.
My heart trips on smooth pavement.
I fall without landing.

Bed is not comforting; sleep is uneven.
I glance to the right in darkness and at dawn,
but you are not there,
no gentle rising and falling
of beloved form beneath the blanket.

Your return is like the sun's rising to a flower.
I turn my face, my being, toward you and absorb your heat.
You nourish me, you comfort me.
You complete me.
My neck, my arms, my chest
revel in your contact,
your remembered form,
the shape, the smell, the breath of you.
You water my parched mouth; the world blooms.

2001

Kiss Kiss

Do you sleep, my love?
Your eyelids flutter slightly
and your breath is soft.
But is it in dreams
or half-waked reverie?
Will you turn toward me
consciously, or unconsciously?
Will you give me a kiss?
Please?
I would sleep better after that.
Or maybe not.

2006

I Would Give You My Heart, But

I would give you my heart, but
it is a bloody thing
and misshapen from the idealized form
by left ventricular hypertrophy
and the usual asymmetry of
sprouting veins and arteries,
of which some on close examination
would show fatty streaks of white
against the proper red,
developing atherosclerosis gifted
by my love of ice cream.

Would you take a ring instead,
round, symmetric, never tarnishing,
plugged only by your finger?

2011

On October 4, 2001

Fifty-five is a good year, a balanced year,
irreversible—the same coming and going,
more than half a century, over double legal age,
still shy of retirement (though AARP eligible)
and a long way from well-wished one hundred and twenty.

You are past child-bearing, but not child caring,
with empty-nesting tasted, but not yet completed,
and bonding still in progress, though now among near equals.
Newly freed to follow work and other interests,
eyes sparkling as you speak with animation
of novel projects, articles, creative gatherings,
at this time you are not reborn, just uncorked,
like a properly matured champagne.

Welcome to your new age, where I have preceded.
Like the back of an inchworm, you have briefly caught up.
I shall go on before you, and ever await you,
and greet you with kisses each year on this day.

2001

The Lump

For your birthday you got a lump.
Well, it had been there for a while
in your right breast,
but you got the report.
Ninety-nine percent chance it's OK,
but there is that niggling one percent.
You've been there before;
you don't want to be Swiss cheese.
It's probably all right, but
this time there are some inconsistencies.
So there should be more tests and more talk,
and, I am sure, more worry.
You sat calmly on our bed
and relayed the information
and we went to sleep.

I will hold you whenever you want.
And then some.

2003

After Thirty-Seven Years

After thirty-seven years,
we still walk hand-in-hand
on Boston streets
or sometimes Cape Cod's sand.

After thirty-seven years,
my heart still gives a leap
at your flashing eyes
or quiet face in sleep.

After thirty-seven years,
the day's somehow amiss
if not completed
with a good-night kiss.

After thirty-seven years
and two children grown,
I know my best friend's
wedding was our own.

2008

Snore

My nighttime vocals,
low and rumbling,
half a snort
and half a steam train,
penetrate her ears
despite the plugs
and toss her from
the shore of sleep
she struggles vainly
once again to reach.
So she tries tugging
lightly on the sheet.
It's not enough
to move or quiet me.
She contemplates
a harder pull,
a desperate—
and not so loving—
pat upon the shoulder.
But miraculously,
there is a lull,
a welcome respite
to send her back to slumber.

Then sometime later
I myself am wakened
by a sweet song,
her gentle whistle,
rising/falling
with her half the sheet.
And so I lie and think:
If only we could sing duets
unheard in sleep.

2009

Middle Ground

This morning when my wife crept softly out
of bed and tiptoed carefully down the hall,
to go to early reiki or the gym,
she left my lumpiness in half-feigned sleep.

I hid there from the coming day's demands
and felt a rush of sybaritic joy
to test the freedom of expanded space—
and moved into the middle of the bed.

Like Leonardo's man I lay
with limbs outstretched,
encountering no barrier
or even reprimand.

How different was this from the nighttime norm
of kiss good night and roll ourselves apart
to hug opposing edges of the bed,
avoiding inadvertent touch till dawn.

I tired at last of lazy solitude
and rose to wait for her with some regret
that I had not awakened more constrained
but with her lying there beside me still.

For though the middle is respected
as a boundary when we sleep,
it sometimes is a joyous place
for us to meet.

2009

Closet Kiss

Searching for a short-sleeved shirt,
I was in the closet,
when she came in, not to flirt,
just to deposit
laundry. But our eyes met.
We kissed and hugged a while
till we were set,
then exited with a quiet smile
the closet underneath the stairs
to return to more mundane affairs.

The moral is this:
A closet kiss
should not be missed
or dissed.

2008

Pajama Pocket

An affectionate pat
on my wife's derriere
surprised me with a jangle
from items stored there:
a pair of her earrings,
a watch-bracelet of glass
that later would gleam
on her figure with class,
but now were carried down
in a rear pajama pocket.
And those who're storage
deficient shouldn't mock it.

2009

Joint Account

The sheet was placed in escrow
with the comforter
there between and over us,
to be withdrawn equally in the night.
Nevertheless, in the morning
I found that I had come up short.
A blanket apology was offered,
but I knew that there would be
just another cover-up.

2013

Low-Lying Blankets

I get up in the night and see
low-lying blankets on the bed,
no Susie-shaped mound that is
my assurance of your presence.
No faint tremors, no sound
of breathing except my own.
The room feels empty—which it is—
and cooler—which it is.
I try to go back to sleep
with only my heat for companionship.
I pull the empty blankets closer.
At least it is just for one night.

2011

Just the Outside

I have seen your body change
from late-teenage girl
to young woman,
all the stages of your pregnancies
and years of motherhood,
through menopause and now
the slow silvering of the hair.
I have loved it all,
for this is the house
in which you dwell.

2011

Entwined from May to May

My arms were made for holding you,
and yours for holding me,
but armless we would still entwine,
like two strands of ivy.

Through forty years of days and nights,
in sun or rainy weather,
we've walked and talked and planned and worked
and slept and waked together.

We raised our children, watched them grow,
move not so far away;
so they will come to celebrate
this 23rd of May

the anniversary of our vows,
exchanging of the rings
that bound us in the big and in
the precious little things.

My lips were made for kissing you,
and yours for kissing me,
but mouthless we would still entwine
like two strands of ivy.

2011

Island

I come downstairs in the middle of the night.
It is so quiet and peaceful.
The refrigerator kicks in for a little while,
but even that is calming,
like the smile of an old friend.
I think how this is an island
in the tumult of the world
and must remember to tell you
and thank you tomorrow,
even when the day's noise has returned.
Here is an island of happiness,
and much of it, for me, is you.

2013

The Bedouin Dress

Forty years ago, when we were young,
we journeyed to Jerusalem. The Old City called us,
so we dropped our bags upon arrival
at our friends', Steve and Paula, there for the year,
and hurried off to walk down ancient cobblestones.
In an alley off the market, a Bedouin dress festooned a wall
and caught our eyes with its rich embroidery,
red and other colors on white handwoven cotton,
muted now by many washings,
and with an old elbow patch further testifying to its age.
It was smaller than its sisters, slender, not the voluminous cut
that could still be worn in pregnancy: a young woman's dress,
perhaps the favored habit of the favored daughter of a chief.
A brilliant smile emerged from the shop across the way;
a glance, and "It will fit her perfectly!" he said.
He ushered us in to coffee we could not refuse;
you tried on the dress—and he was right.
Then came the bargaining, one-sided since I knew
that I had left the money with our bags.
At last, embarrassed, I showed him the meager contents of my wallet,
little more than forty dollars and some change,
plus two Israeli telephone tokens from our friends,
in case we had to call.
With great delight he took it all and with a flourished hand
gave back—one telephone token, and the dress.

It does not matter that the dress now sleeps in the closet;
I still have my memories of it
and of you emerging gloriously from the fitting room,
in Jerusalem, where my grandfather was born.

2013

A Good Walk

Two paths ran through the woods,
over hills and alongside streams,
crossed, diverged and crossed again,
and finally met and merged.
And we two walkers in the woods,
once on separate tracks,
having kissed and walked away and kissed again,
now walk hand in hand,
steadying each other's stumbles;
knowing there were other paths,
we look into each other's eyes
and smile.

2011

Why Flesh and Blood?

Why make a world of flesh and blood
atop the rock and within the seas?
Why make a world of flesh and blood,
with all its hurts and cuts and pains?
Why not something else instead,
like beings of gas that float on high
or beings of rock that never bleed?

Oh, they too arose in the mind of God,
and they were created with a Word
to float or tumble in their own space.
But this world, this world is ours.

Gas beings in pairs
merge and separate
and then extrude
buds that break away and float
along their own trajectories,
while crystalline folk
slough off their young
in chips and bits that recombine
along the facets and the vertices.

And you and I,
we too merge and separate,
and I left a piece of me with you
to grow another being of flesh.

But you have also left
a piece of you in me,
ethereal as a gas globe
and yet of such rocklike solidity
to be the fulcrum for the rod
that moves the universe for me.

2012

Daughters

I have two daughters,
fair of face,
bright of spirit,
minds like prisms,
bringing forth colors
and rays of imagination;
strong willed and demanding of self,
tempestuous over injustice;
steadfast with friends—and these well chosen—
yet whole in solitude, at ease with quiet.

I have two daughters:
one leaping, rushing to the bell
or the drum.
A wind follows her, surrounds her, pushes at us in her wake;
a gust may carry us along joyfully,
or sometimes leave us picking up small debris.
The glint of the kitten, playing with life's string, flashes in her eyes.
Her inspiration is song and legend centuries old.
Her fingers build noncorporeal images
in recorder notes and computer code.

I have two daughters:
one moves in quiet deliberation,
nurturing, supporting self and others,
with an occasional avalanche footfall,
a brief geyser of inner boil.
She will cook to eat, and to feed.
She now builds mostly with words but intends
good things for people to live in
and appreciate.
She knows the value of the spice in cooking and architecture.

I have two daughters
whose sum is greater than their separate infinities.
Each enlivens and strengthens the other
through both their similarities and their differences,
in close friendship as well as sisterhood.
And I, though not quite content,
on due consideration
am nearly so
and must remember to tell them of my great happiness in them.

I have two wonderful daughters.

1994

KENDRA

Knowing your past, hoping your future,
  Eighteen years we have watched you grow, unfold.
    New paths open, in sunshine and shadow.
      Daughter of mine, now and forever,
        Remember where you have walked, but look
        Ahead.

1993

Graduation Day 1997

Kendra—the spark we kindled
and fed soft moss, then twigs, then branches,
now burns brightly, gloriously,
leaping upwards; still young
but strong with confident hope and promise.
A Yule log from a summer's day.

Hugs are more equal now,
and soon comes the gentle metamorphosis
from inhabitant to cherished visitor.

My child but your self;
your parent, but may I say, your friend.
Bonds loosened and bonds tightened.

On this day, I too graduate.

1997

Thirty-Three
(for Kendra)

In two ways you're now a product of primes:
Your age, 33, is 3 eleven times,
and you are our prima in old Roman style
as we were our parents' in ranking their file.
(Or would the declension have made us two "primi"?
Well, whatever works to make the poem rhymy.)
On this your new birthday we fondly attest,
of all the first daughters we love you the best.
And we really like the way that you grew:
You're in your prime, and the prime's in you.

2008

To Kendra at Thirty-Seven

Thirty-seven is
another prime year
to cap off with wishes
from those you hold dear
for a year full of love,
a year of great passion
and wire-work wonders
we know you will fashion
out of your spirit,
out of your soul.
For some spin their lives,
some give it a roll,
but you give it curves
and spirals fantastic.
Ethereal pliers,
not a wand, works your magic.

2012

6-12
(for Kendra)

For most of my generation,
6-12 means the bug spray,
that most effective weapon
in the war against mosquitoes,
the protective film that covered us,
at least in hope,
rubbed on hands and necks
and behind the ears
before we strolled into the woods
or merely braved the backyard barbecue.
But for me the phrase 6-12
is life-affirming, full of promise,
for it is the birthday of you, my firstborn,
once a beautiful baby and now a woman.
Your wails of yesteryear that proclaimed
to me and to the world, "I am here!"
are now measured and thoughtful words
and smiles and hugs of greeting that convey
we both are here and happy for it.
So when the year has rolled
through half the months it has,
and flying, biting things have reappeared,
I'm reminded that 6-12 is just my code
to wish you Happy Birthday once again.

2013

For Your Wedding

For your wedding,
conventional and unconventional,
there were six groomsmen dressed in black,
but two were women.

For your wedding,
there were six bridesmaids dressed in blue;
four were svelte and smiling,
and two were heavy with their fruit and smiling more.

For your wedding,
you wore white, but leather
from the high-back collar to your hips,
embroidered and silver buttoned at the front
and laced down the sides,
with a flowing silk skirt below.

For your wedding,
the flowers were rosebuds of blues,
but wooden, to last almost forever,
like your bond.

2013

Wedding Day

My daughter, to reach this day
you have slain the dragons of uncertainty,
or at least kept them at bay,
whittled them down to manageable size
with the twin swords of your mind and your heart.

This is the day you wed your beloved.
He should love you forever, as I do, though differently.
I have loved you in all your incarnations,
as a baby, as a girl child, as a young woman.
He has known you only as a woman.
He should love you as the half of himself
that he has finally found.

I do not give you away today;
you give yourself, as he gives himself,
and together you will be stronger.
We are delighted to share you and to share in him.

It is not that you leave my house this day;
you have had your own for quite some time.
It is you who invited him in,
into your house and into your heart,
though we welcome him, too.

You do not go to a distant castle,
across rivers and mountains,
barriers of topography or of the heart.
I hope the two of you will always find
the way easy to our door.

2013

KYLA

Kisses sent from smiling eyes,
Youthfully shy, but calm and wise,
Lounging best with a full bookshelf,
Always faithful both to friends and self.

1994

Blue-Eyed Bundle
(for Kyla)

My blue-eyed bundle,
that was you,
staring so intently
back at me
in the recovery room
at Boston Lying-In.
Others' mothers surrounded us,
also stared at the two of us,
and clearly wondered where
we'd stashed yours
(temporarily, thank goodness).

It's now 8-8 of 2008,
such a balanced date.
Twenty-nine years have passed,
and you're a poised professional,
blue-eyed still,
with close-cropped hair
and earring elegance,
making history in the retelling
at Back Bay's Gibson House;
and in the summertime,
keeping kids in line
(in SPACE* and script);
and chasing rapper teammates
round and round
in complicated weaves
and finally flipping out, or in.

You're grown, and now
you're someone else's
blue-eyed bundle, too.
You're still mine
to hold at times.
but I will leave
the carrying to him with pride.

2008

*Newton schools' Summer Program for Academic and Creative Encounters. Kyla was a counselor and then assistant director for musical theater for many years.

May You Grow Old in Love
(for Kyla)

May you grow old in love, my child,
with your love by your side.
May you grow old together,
bound in love and friendship and smiles.
May your love grow from young love to old love,
from flames to embers still glowing.
May you hold each other more tightly
and still dance when the beat is slowing.

2006

Baby Bellies
(for Kyla)

Thirty years ago it was your baby belly
that I tickled with my nose
and blew rude noises in
to your peals of laughter
and then bright eyes of anticipation
when I stopped for the first time,
or second, or third.
Now you have a baby belly
swollen with pride and promise.
And I know that I had better
soften up my nose
and practice trumpeting
rude noises on my arm
in my own bright-eyed anticipation
of a return performance
on a new venue.

2011

On First Holding My Grandson

Wrapped in his blanket,
with just his head revealed,
an ovoid still elongated from its journey
and covered at least for now with long dark hair,
he lay quietly,
with small tremors of breath and potential,
sleeping before the insistent yell.
There was a weight to him—
more than his seven pounds, fourteen ounces—
of histories mingled,
hope and promise,
and my joy.

2011

Zichri Berel*

Your name is Remembrance,
to remind us
while we are still here,
and to be the rememberer
of these things
when we are gone.
You will be the vessel
and the liquid,
the rock
and the inscription,
the voice
and the song,
and you will hold our line
and preserve us in memory,
as we have held you
and sheltered you
from these your first days
to as long as our strength lasts.

2011

*My Memory of Berel; Berel was Susan's father's Hebrew name.

Motherhood Suits You

Motherhood suits you,
well, we knew it would,
you who told me when I asked
what you wanted your friends to bring you
for presents at your first real birthday party,
at age three—"A baby!"
You who wanted dolls more than stuffed animals,
though you sat high on the life-sized St. Bernard
or on rainbow-colored Puff the Magic Dragon;
babies and children were your thing.
You the early reader to your peers,
seated attentively in a circle around you;
a children's Shakespeare's tales was a favorite.

And now you have your own little one
who toddles round in mutual entertainment;
he too gets stories and different kinds of food,
and you get "Mango?"
and the muttered "Not plan,"
the product of an escaped glop upon his pants.
We watch the interactions in delight
and conclude that at nearly two years
you are both well trained.

2013

Thunder Stick

THUMP. THUMP. THUMP.
Great-grandma's cane climbs the stairs…
THUMP. THUMP. THUMP.
up to the door on the second floor…
THUMP. THUMP. THUMP.
where Zed peeks out…
THUMP. THUMP. THUMP.
held aloft in his daddy's hands.
THUMP. THUMP. THUMP.
Great-grandma comes in and sits.
"Stick," says Zed.
"Yes, that is great-grandma's stick, or cane."
"Hole," says Zed.
"Yes, there is a hole in the end of the handle."
"Stick," says Zed.
He holds the cane by its middle.
It is as tall as he is.
He tries it out:
Thump. Thump. Thump.
Thunder stick!

2013

Bequests to My Children

I bequeath you my dreams,
not for yourselves,
for you have your own dreams,
but to remember me.

I bequeath you my deeds,
the good ones for inspiration,
the bad ones for warnings
and inspiration to find another way.

Remember me with humor
and tolerance for my failings.
Remember my love.

I do not bequeath you my love;
I gave it to you long ago.

2014

About the Author

Keith Tornheim is a biochemistry professor at Boston University School of Medicine. He was a co-winner of a Great Lakes College Association poetry contest in 1967 and is now a relapsed poet, with poems appearing in *Poetica, Ibbetson Street, Boston Literary Magazine, Muddy River Poetry Review* and *Lyrical Somerville (The Somerville News/Times)*. His poems have been a part of High Holiday and other services of his congregation (see *www.shirhadash-ma.org/poetry.html*). In recent years, conversations with dancer/choreographer Wendy Jehlen on her developing Lilith composition led to the writing of a poem cycle on the story of Lilith, the first consort of Adam. This instigated another poem cycle, *Spoiled Fruit: Adam and Eve in Eden and Beyond*, recently published by Poetica Publishing. He lives in Newton Highlands, Massachusetts, with his wife, Susan, a fiber artist and his primary critic and copy editor. Their daughters, sons-in-law and grandson live two towns away.

www.ingramcontent.com/pod-product-compliance
Lightning Source LLC
LaVergne TN
LVHW091321080426
835510LV00007B/588